Crazy Puppets

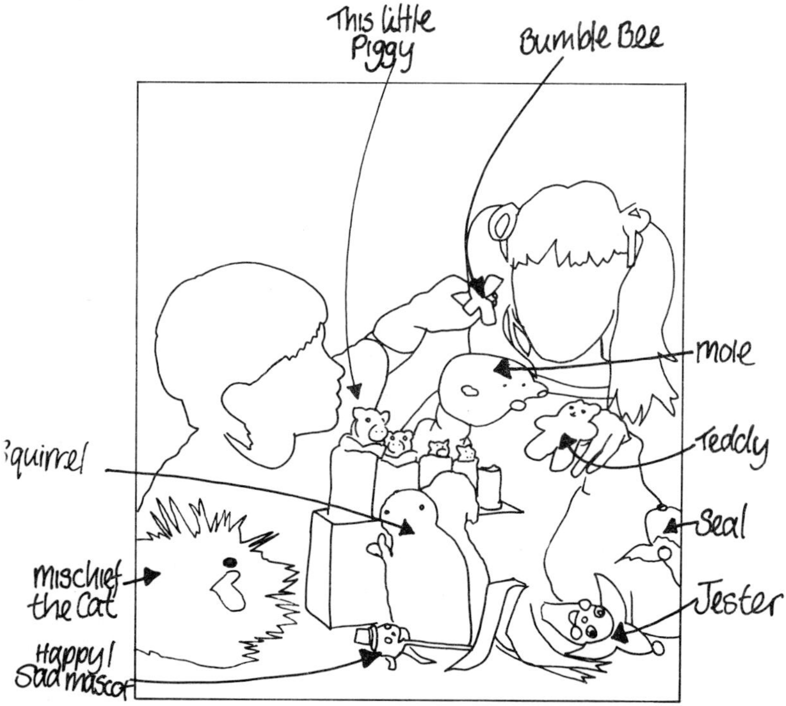

key to front cover photograph

key to back cover photograph

Crazy Puppets
Delphine Evans

*Designed by Jane Laycock
Illustrated by Jane Laycock
and Sheila McGee*

HUTCHINSON
London   Melbourne   Auckland   Johannesburg

Copyright © Delphine Evans 1987
Copyright © Illustrations Century Hutchinson Ltd 1987

All rights reserved

First published in 1987 by Hutchinson Children's Books
An imprint of Century Hutchinson Ltd
Brookmount House, 62–65 Chandos Place,
Covent Garden, London WC2N 4NW

Century Hutchinson Australia Pty Ltd
16–22 Church Street, Hawthorn, Melbourne, Victoria 3122

Century Hutchinson New Zealand Limited
32–34 View Road, PO Box 40–086, Glenfield, Auckland 10

Century Hutchinson South Africa (Pty) Ltd
PO Box 337, Bergvlei 2012, South Africa

Set in Times by BookEns, Saffron Walden, Essex

Printed and bound in Great Britain by Anchor Brendon Ltd,
Tiptree, Essex

British Library Cataloguing in Publication Data

Evans, Delphine
 Crazy puppets.
 1. Puppet making — Juvenile literature
 I. Title   II. Laycock, Jane
 III. McGee, Shelagh
 745.592'24   TT174.7

ISBN 0–09–17810–4

Contents

Introduction 9

Making your Crazy Puppets 10
Materials 10
Tools 12
Hints and Tips on Making Your Puppets 13
Hints and Tips on Using Your Puppets 18

Finger Puppets 20
●● Dalmatian 20
● Man With a Nose That Grows 22
● Bumble Bee 24
● Ladybird 27
● Fish Finger 29
● Dragonfly 31
● Trumper the Elephant 33

Hand Puppets 36
●●● Tish Tissue 36
●●● Fish Bag 37
●●● Seal 39
●●● Baa Baa Black Sheep 40
●● Cat and Kitten Mitten 41
● Two-faced Clown 43
● Hedgehog 46
● Mole 50
● Squirrel 54

Stick Puppets 59
●●● Lipstick Baby 59

●●● Crazy Spider 62
●●● Safety Sticks 64
●●● Jester Spoon 65
●●   Happy/Sad Mascot 67
●●   Pop-up Baby 70
●●   Chicken Inside an Egg 72
●   Growing Flowers 75
●   This Little Piggy 79

Walking Puppets 83
●●   Humpty Dumpty 83
●●   Teddy 87

Special Puppets 90
●●● Pen Pal 90
●●   Mischief the Cat 93

Introduction

Puppets are fun to make and fun to use!

In this book you will find puppets of all shapes and sizes for you to make. Some you sew together; some you glue. Some are from odds and ends; some are from new materials. Some are quick and easy; some are harder and take a little longer to make. All of them are fun!

The dots by each puppet show how hard it is to make. One dot means it's very easy; two mean medium; three for when you've had some practice and are a bit more confident. Ask an adult to help you with the more difficult puppets. It's probably a good idea to start with the easy puppets and gradually work your way through to the harder ones.

Then when you have made your puppets, there are ideas on how to use them to get your imagination working. After that it's up to you. I hope you enjoy it!

Making your Crazy Puppets

Materials

You can make puppets from almost anything. If you intend making quite a few it's a good idea to start a Bitbox (for small bits) and a Scrapstore (for larger items).

Bitbox

For your Bitbox you will need a box or tin with a lid. Collect and keep inside it small bits and pieces which will be useful for your puppets' features, and any other little decorations. Remember that quality is more important than quantity.

Suggested bits and pieces

Sequins, buttons, beads, small shells – for eyes and noses
Bits of fur, wool, string, raffia, cotton wool, feathers – for whiskers and hair
Short pieces of lace, ribbon, tinsel – for decoration
Oddments of felt, pretty material, paper, foil – for decoration

Scrapstore

For your Scrapstore you will need either a large cardboard box or a special shelf or cupboard. Collect and keep any old and used items that will be suitable for puppet heads, bodies, arms and legs.

Suggested scraps

Empty cardboard containers from tissues, cereals and toothpaste
Matchboxes and round cheese boxes
Egg boxes, lolly sticks, yoghurt pots, milk and cream containers, lipstick tubes and spatulas
Old socks, tights, mittens, gloves and handkerchiefs
Different types and thicknesses of paper, including tissue, gummed paper and wallpaper
Paper bags, rubber bands and cotton reels
Plastic tubes and containers
Wooden and plastic spoons, dish mops, used felt-tip pens and biros and broken knitting needles
Old rubber or polystyrene balls or other round objects suitable for heads
Oddments of fur, felt and pretty pieces of cotton material

New materials

The new materials which have been used in this book are all easily obtainable in stores or craft shops. Markets are another good source. When you're out shopping, look around to see what's available, then you will know where to go when you need the items.

Suggested new materials

Joggle eyes
Plastic noses, mouths, whiskers and paws
Pipe cleaners (including glitter ones)
Sticks (used pencil or felt-tip pen will do)
Bells
Felt squares and fur fabric
Stuffing (you can cut up old tights)
Polystyrene balls

Tools

The tools required depend on which puppet you decide to make. The following list covers all the puppets in the book.

Felt-tip pens
Pencil
Ruler or tape measure
Pins or safety pins
Needle
Cotton
Glue
Paper of different sizes
Cardboard
Carbon paper
Tracing paper (or greaseproof paper)

Hints and Tips on Making Your Puppets

Gluing

1. It is important to use the correct type of glue; particularly when sticking plastic and polystyrene. Read the label carefully to avoid disappointing results.

2. Don't put on too much glue – it's surprising how little you need.

3. Try not to glue too big an area at a time –especially when it's curved or has an uneven surface. Press from the middle outwards to avoid air bubbles.

4. Have patience and wait for the glue to set properly.

5. If you take it step by step and follow the instructions you should have no problems.

Sewing seams

Small running stitches can be used for seams. Follow the instructions below.

1. Put the right sides of your work together.

2. To make sure the edges stay evenly together, use pins or safety pins at intervals along the edge to be sewn.

3. Choose a matching cotton. Thread your needle and tie a knot at the end.

4. Starting at the right-hand edge, draw the needle from the back to the front through both pieces of material.

5. Leave a short space and take the needle through to the back and continue to go in and out making small running stitches until the seam is finished. Take out your pins as you reach them.

6. Fasten off securely by sewing over the last stitch several times.

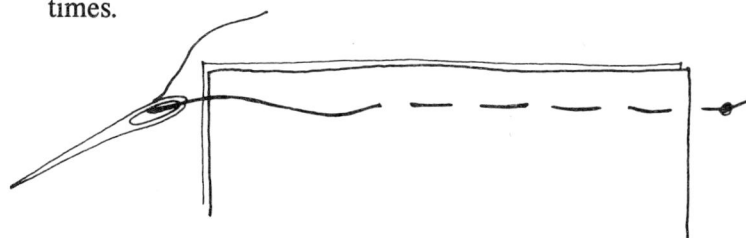

Gathering material

Repeat as for *Sewing seams* (3–5), but your stitches can be longer ones.

6. Pull the cotton until the material is sufficiently gathered.

7. Fasten off securely by sewing over the last stitch several times.

8. Make sure your gathers are evenly spaced.

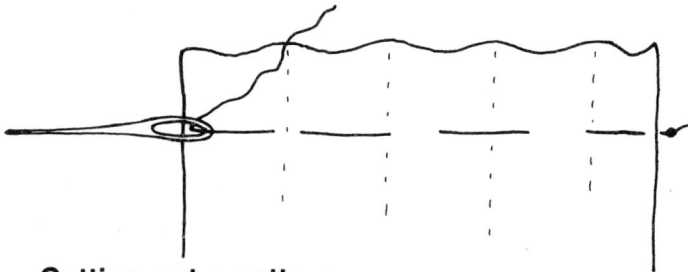

Cutting out a pattern

1. If the pattern instructs you to cut one of a particular pattern piece, pin the pattern piece to the wrong side of your material and cut out.

2. If the pattern instructs you to cut two of a particular pattern piece, fold your material in half, wrong sides together, before pinning the pattern piece in place and cutting out.

3. If the pattern instructs you to cut four of a particular pattern piece, fold your material in half, wrong sides together, pin your pattern piece in place and cut out, then pin your pattern piece in place again and cut out.

Enlarging a pattern

Whenever you see a pattern drawn on a grid you will usually read, 'Enlarge the pattern to the right size on a piece of A4 paper'.

1. You will need a piece of A4 paper approximately 30 x 21 cm.

2. Divide it into the same number of rectangles as the grid shown in the book.

3. Redraw the pattern, copying one rectangle at a time into the corresponding rectangle on your piece of paper.

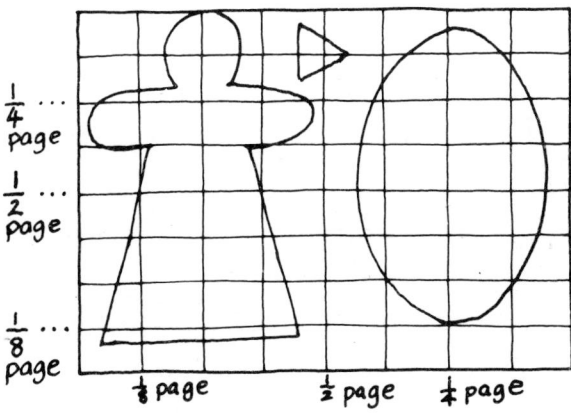

Tracing

For some of the puppets you can trace the diagram and use your tracing paper as a pattern. To do this, pin the tracing to your material or paper and cut around it.

For other puppets you will need to transfer the tracing to either cardboard or paper. To do this you will need tracing paper (or greaseproof paper), carbon paper, and a pencil.

1. Cover the diagram with the tracing paper and draw the outline on to it.

2. Place your tracing over the cardboard (or whatever you wish to trace the diagram on to).

3. Place a piece of carbon paper face down between your tracing and the cardboard.

4. Follow the outline which you have made on your tracing paper – covering every line and pressing firmly.

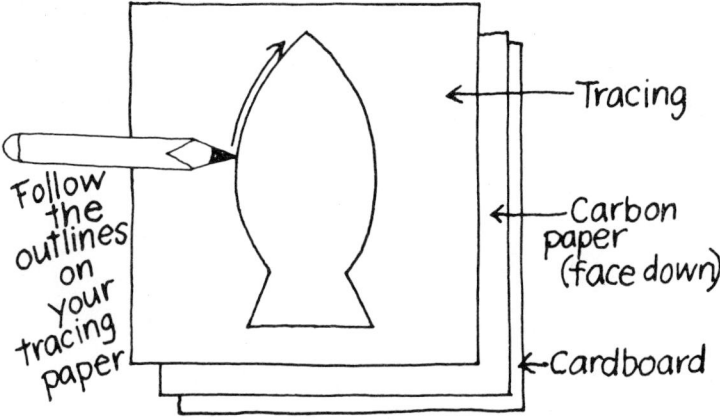

5. You will find that you have made an accurate copy of the diagram.

How to begin

1. Decide which puppet you want to make and read through the instructions carefully before you begin.

2. Collect together all the materials and tools you will need.

3. Now you're ready. Start at the beginning and work through the instructions step by step. You will be surprised how easy it is and how much fun you will have!

Hints and Tips on Using Your Puppets

Name your puppet

Look at him and move him about. A name will almost certainly spring to mind. Some of the puppets in the book are already named – like Tish who's made from tissues, Trumper the elephant and Mischief the cat.

A name turns an object into a character. You need a name and so does your puppet.

How to use your finger puppets

Finger puppets are the easiest of all puppets to use, because as soon as you put one on your finger and wiggle it – it comes alive.

Think as the character on your finger thinks: a dragonfly might think, 'I see something near the ground I'd like to look at', and swoop down. Then quick as a flash he decides to fly back upwards again! If you have made a puppet of an animal or bird, watch the natural movements of the real animal or bird and copy them as closely as possible. This will make your puppet look realistic.

How to use your hand and arm puppets

Never hold your hand in the air to show off an animal puppet – have you ever seen an animal suspended in mid air? Use your lap if you are sitting down or, if you are standing up, rest the puppet on your other arm. Make your puppet sit or climb on objects that are around.

Think like the animal and imitate its actions as closely as possible. If he's a squirrel, make him run very quickly up your arm; put a nut between his paws and make him nibble it.

Finger Puppets

● Dalmatian

You will need

White cardboard 5 x 5 cm
Black and red felt-tip pens
Scissors

Instructions

1. Trace the dalmatian's head on to cardboard and cut out along both heavy cutting lines.

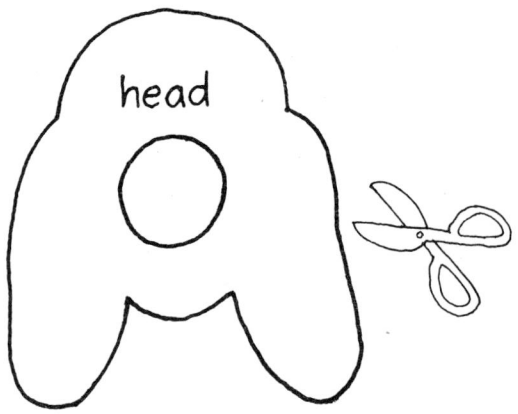

2. Draw two eyes just above the circle.

3. Colour with black dalmatian spots.

4. Draw a black nose and red tongue on the end of your middle finger.

How to use

Put your middle finger through the hole, to make the dog's head.

You have three fingers and a thumb to use as legs. Make your dog nod his head, walk and sit.

● Man With a Nose That Grows

You will need

Cardboard
Felt-tip pens
Scissors

Instructions

1. Trace the man on to the cardboard and cut out along all heavy cutting lines.

2. Colour him in.

How to use

Put your finger slowly through the hole, so that his nose gradually becomes longer.

Give him a name, and say, 'I am ..... with a nose, that grows – and grows – and grows!

● Bumble Bee

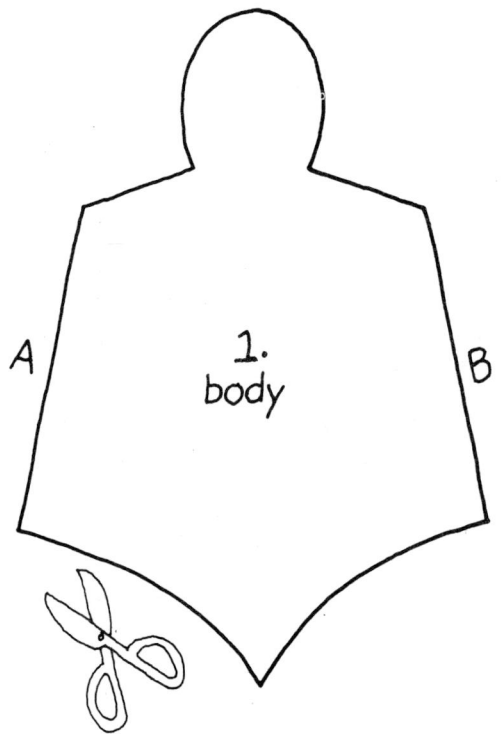

You will need

White paper
Glue
Black and yellow felt-tip pens

Instructions

1. Trace shapes **1** and **2** on to plain paper and cut out.

A 1. body B

2. Colour the body **1** with thick black stripes and the wings **2** with black and yellow lines as shown.

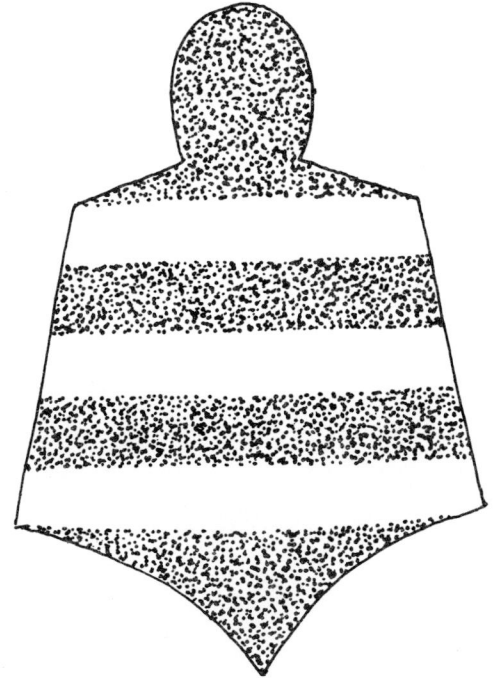

3. Glue along lines **A** and **B** and make a tube to fit your finger.

4. Glue the centre of the wings to the tube.

5. Cut out two feelers, colour them black and glue them into place.

How to use

Make your bumble bee buzz about, like a real one!

● Ladybird

You will need

Paper
Felt-tip pens
Tracing paper
Glue

Instructions

1. Trace shapes **1** and **2** on to your paper and cut out.

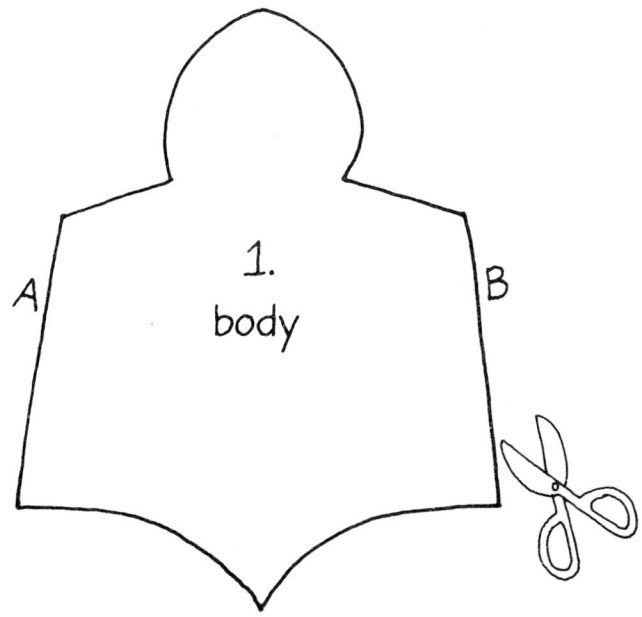

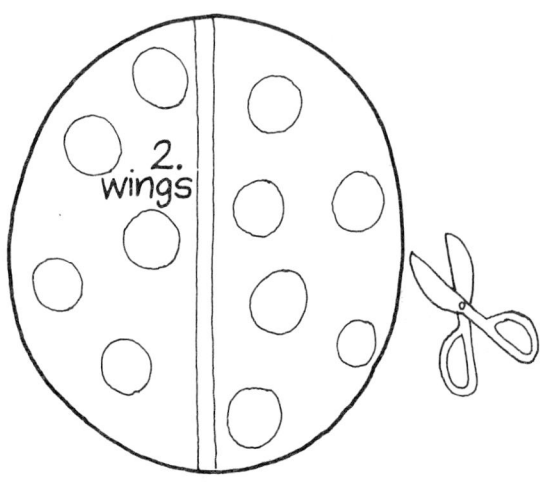

2. Colour the body **1** black and the wings **2** red with black spots.

3. Glue sides **A** and **B** of body **1** together.

4. Glue the centre of the wings **2** to the centre of the body **1**.

How to use

Imitate the movements of a ladybird as she flies from leaf to leaf.

● Fish Finger

You will need

2 pieces of paper or felt 10 x 5 cm
Glue
Scissors
Felt-tip pens (for paper fish)
Sequins (for felt fish)

Instructions

1. Trace the fish shape on to both pieces of paper and cut out. Or use the tracing as a pattern and cut out two shapes in felt.

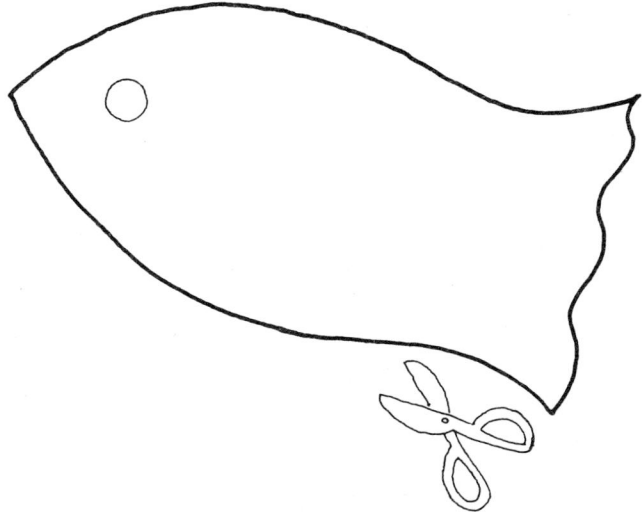

2. Glue the sides together leaving the end of the tail open.

3. If you are making the paper fish, draw in the eyes and scales.

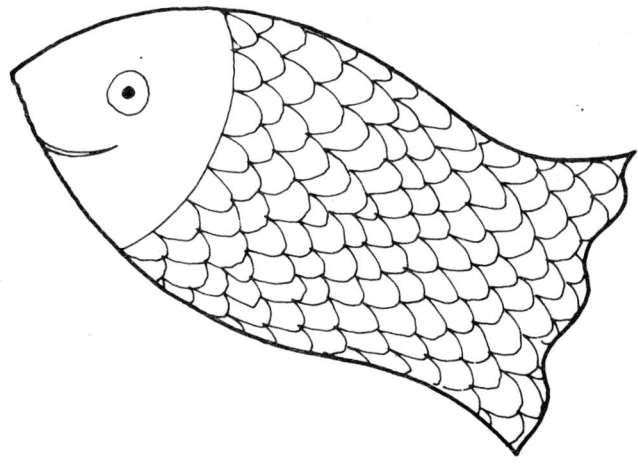

4. If you are making the felt fish, glue on sequins to make eyes and scales.

How to use

Put him on your first finger and wiggle him about. Hide him away and ask your friends if they've ever seen a fish finger they can't eat – then wriggle yours in front of them!

● Dragonfly

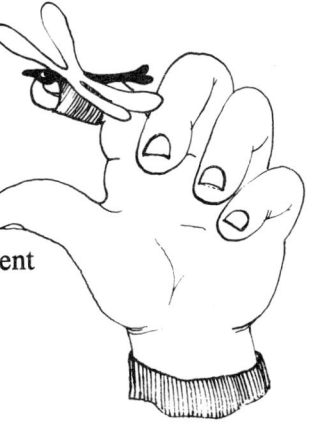

You will need

2 pieces of tissue paper, different colours
Black paper
Glue

Instructions

1. Trace shapes **1** and **2** on to black paper and cut out. These will form the body.

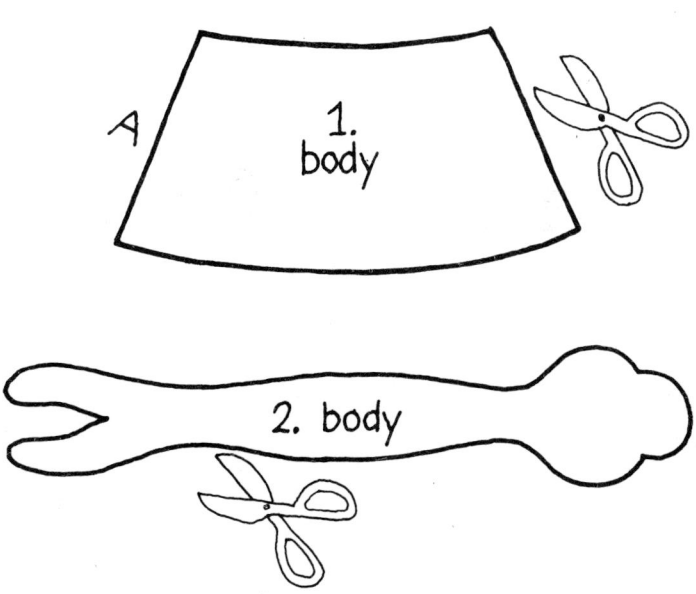

2. Trace shape **3** on to two pieces of tissue paper and cut out. These will form the wings.

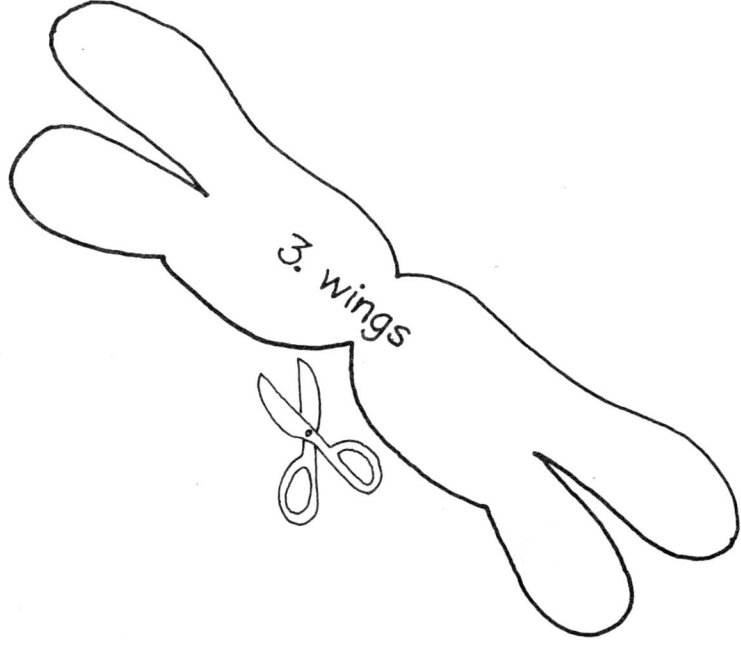

3. Glue along edge **A** of body **1** and make into a tube to fit your finger.

4. Glue centre of wings to body **2**.

5. Glue body **2** to body **1**.

6. Your dragonfly is ready to use.

How to use

Make him dart about quickly – just like a real dragonfly.

●●Trumper the Elephant

You will need

Grey felt 14 x 9 cm
Oddments of green, pink and white felt
Glue
Scissors

Instructions

1. Trace shape **1** and, using the tracing as a pattern, cut two from the grey felt.

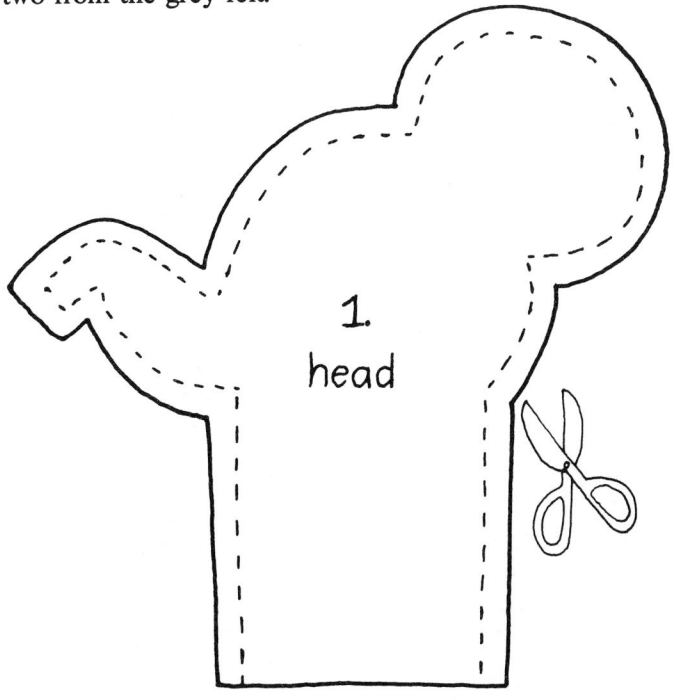

2. Glue around edges as shown by dotted line.

3. Press together.

4. Trace shapes **2, 3, 4** and **5** and use the tracings as patterns.

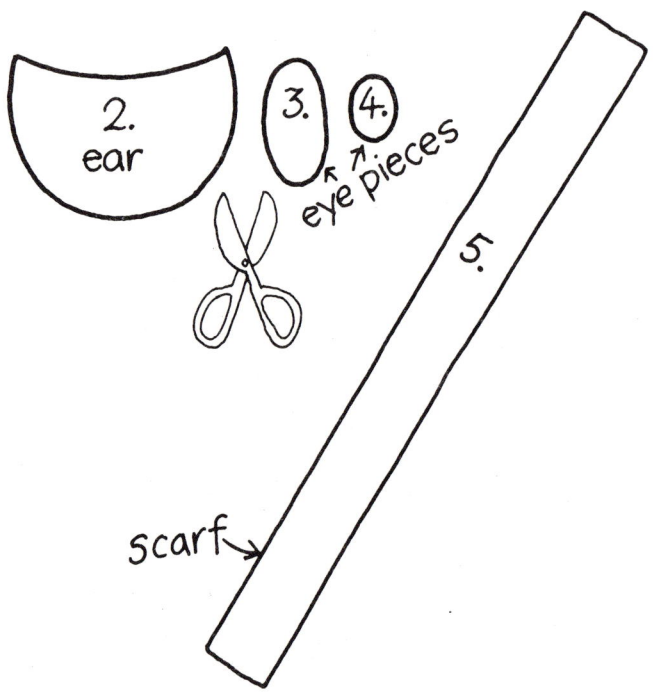

5. Cut out shape **2** twice, using pink felt, to make ears.

6. Cut out shape **3** twice, using pink felt, and shape **4** twice, using white felt, to make eyes.

7. Cut out shape **5** using green felt, to make scarf.

8. Glue in position.

How to use

Put Trumper on your finger and make elephant noises.

Hand Puppets

● Tish Tissue

You will need

Tissue
3 elastic bands
Felt-tip pen

Instructions

1. Fold the tissue across diagonally.

2. Hold up your hand with fingers outstretched.

3. Cover them with the tissue

4. Put an elastic band over the tissue on to your thumb (to make an arm), another band on your middle three fingers (for the head) and the last one on your little finger (for the other arm).

5. Draw a face on the tissue.

6. Your Tish Tissue is ready to use.

How to use

Make him nod his head, wave his arms and clap his hands.

● Fish Bag

You will need

Paper bag
Felt-tip pens
Elastic band

Instructions

1. Open out bag and twist both corners of the bottom edge at **A** and **B** as shown.

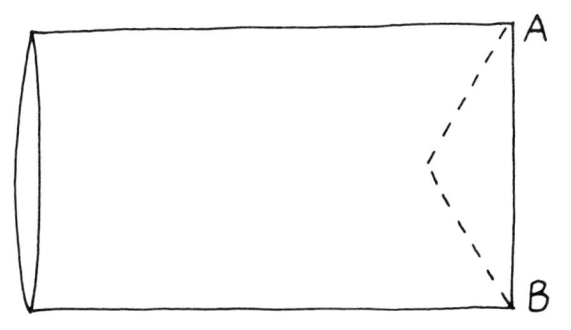

2. Draw on two large eyes as shown.

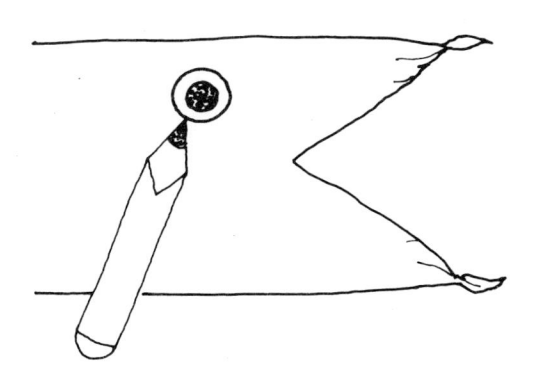

3. Put the bag on your hand, placing your fingers in the top of the jaw and your thumb in the bottom.

4. Place an elastic band around your wrist to secure the fish in place.

How to use

Open and close his mouth and make swimming movements like a real fish.

Find fishy rhymes to use.

● Seal

You will need

Old sock
Bright buttons
Dull button
Wool for whiskers
Glue

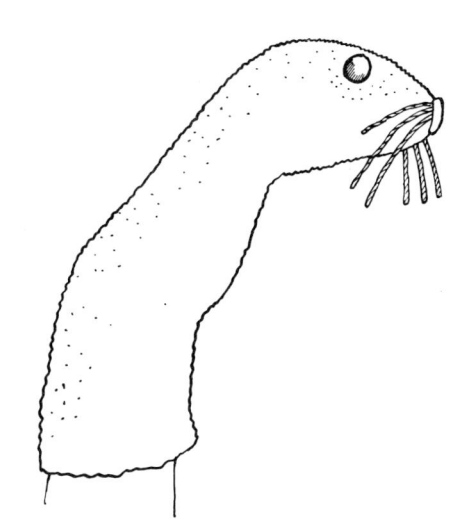

Instructions

1. Glue the dull button in the middle of the toe end of the sock.

2. Glue the wool whiskers each side of the button.

3. Glue the bright buttons in place for eyes.

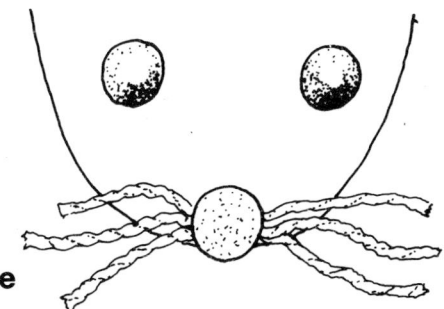

How to use

Put your hand inside and make him move his head up and down.

Seals love playing with balls, so find a ball and attach some string to it. Hold it out for your seal to play with. Cut out a cardboard hoop for him to jump through.

● Baa Baa Black Sheep

You will need

Glove
Oddments of felt, black wool or fur
Felt-tip pens
Glue
Scissors

Instructions

1. To make your black sheep, cut fur or wool and glue on to the thumb of the glove.

2. Cut three bag shapes from felt, and glue on to three fingers of the glove.

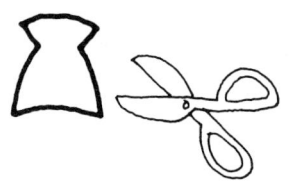

3. Cut the top from the little finger of the glove.

4. Put on the glove.

5. Draw a face on your little finger.

How to use

Curl up all the fingers and pop them up as the rhyme suggests.

●●Cat and Kitten Mitten

You will need

Mitten
Fur and felt oddments
Pipe cleaner
2 large eyes
Glue or needle and cotton
Scissors

Instructions

1. Cut the fur into strips and glue or sew to the mitten to make the face outlines as in the illustration.

2. Cut noses out of fur for the cat and kitten and glue them in place.

3. Trace shapes **1**, **2** and **3**, and, using the tracings as patterns, cut two of each shape from felt.

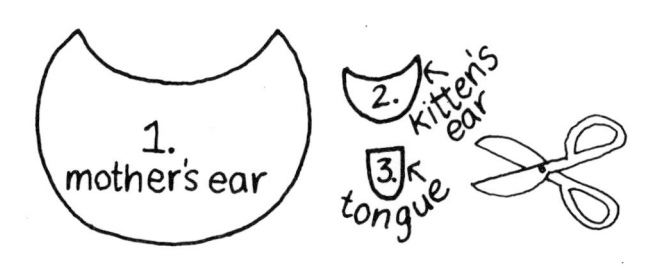

1. mother's ear

2. kitten's ear

3. tongue

4. Glue the ears and tongue in position on the cat and kitten.

5. Make the pipe cleaner into a long tail for the cat and a short one for the kitten. Push the ends through the mitten, and knot, so they are kept in place. Glue a piece of fur to the end of each tail.

6. Make bows from felt for the cat and kitten and glue them in position.

7. Make eyes, nose and whiskers from oddments and glue in place.

How to use

Look out for rhymes about cats like 'Pussy cat, pussy cat'. You can make your kitten shy by hiding him behind the cat and gradually letting him peep out.

●●● Two-faced Clown

You will need

Round cheese box with lid
2 different pieces of
 material 15 x 25 cm
Matchbox cover
Oddments of wool (for hair)
Felt, coloured paper, beads
 and sequins (for features)
Glue
Sellotape

Instructions

1. Cut a hole through the rim of the cheese box and lid to fit the matchbox cover as shown.

2. Glue the matchbox cover into position.

3. Tape the lid securely to the cheese box.

4. Make up two sets of features from as many different oddments as possible, one happy and one sad.

5. Glue into place on either side of the box as shown.

6. Give your puppet woollen hair, using a different colour on each side.

7. Put the two pieces of material together and cut a dress shape (as shown).

8. Glue your two dress shapes together along the edges shown by dotted lines.

9. Ease the neck end around the matchbox and glue into place.

10. Cut out two felt hands, and two bow ties of different colours.

11. Glue the hands into place, and glue one bow tie to each side of the puppet.

How to use

Put your hand inside the puppet and twist him about – showing first one side, then the other. Ask your friends to compare both sides and spot the differences.

● ● ● Hedgehog

You will need

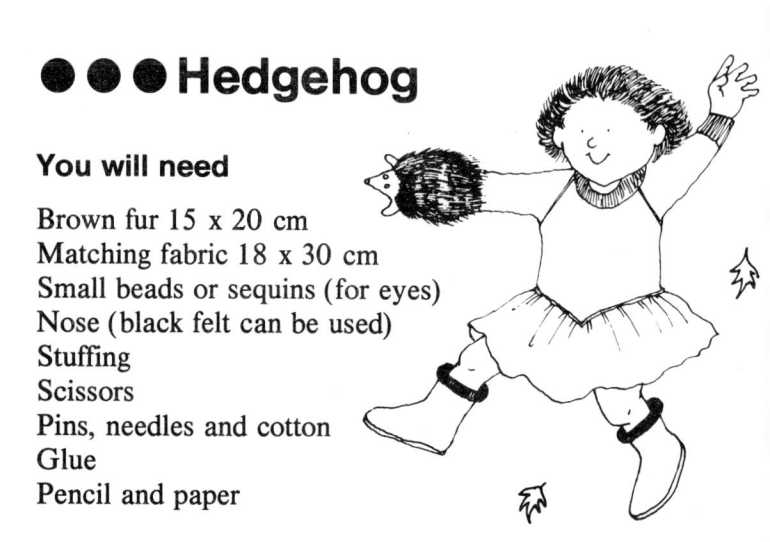

Brown fur 15 x 20 cm
Matching fabric 18 x 30 cm
Small beads or sequins (for eyes)
Nose (black felt can be used)
Stuffing
Scissors
Pins, needles and cotton
Glue
Pencil and paper

Instructions

1. Enlarge the pattern to the right size on a piece of A4 paper and cut it out (see page 15).

2. Place the pattern pieces on the material as follows:
   1 and **4** on the fur
   2 and **3** on the fabric.

3. Pin in place and cut out one of **1**, two of **2**, two of **3** and one of **4** (see page 14).

4. Put the two hand pieces **3** together, turn inside out and sew around the edges, leaving straight edge **A** open.

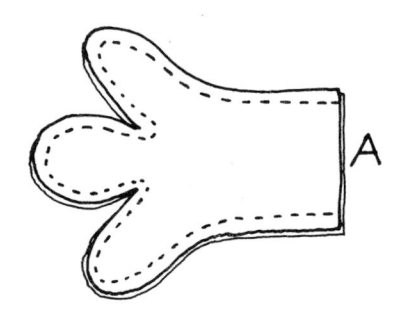

1. back

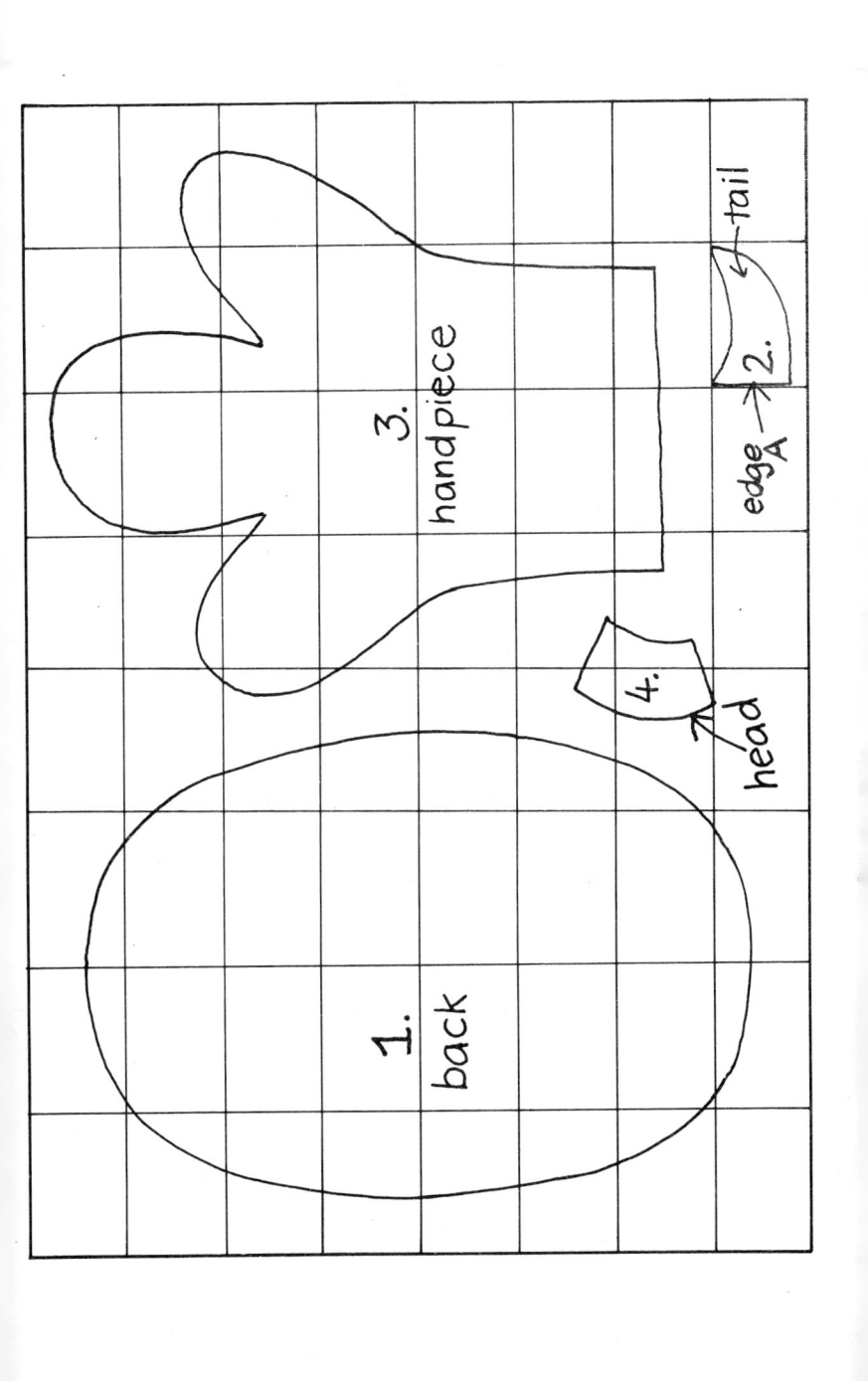

3. handpiece

4. head

2. tail

edge A

5. Turn right side out.

6. Gather the fur piece **1** as shown, to make it fit on to the hand piece leaving the legs and head free.

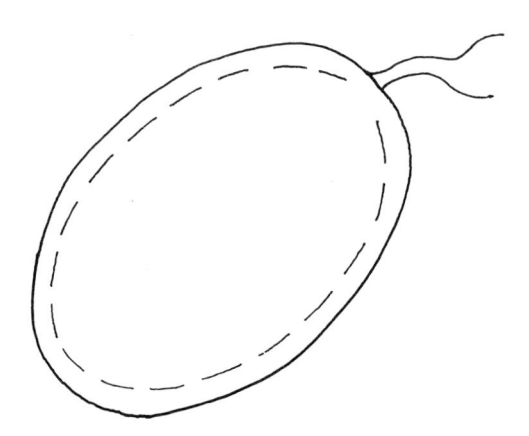

7. Sew the fur on to the hand piece (taking care only to sew through the top layer of the hand piece). Just before you finish, stuff the fur slightly.

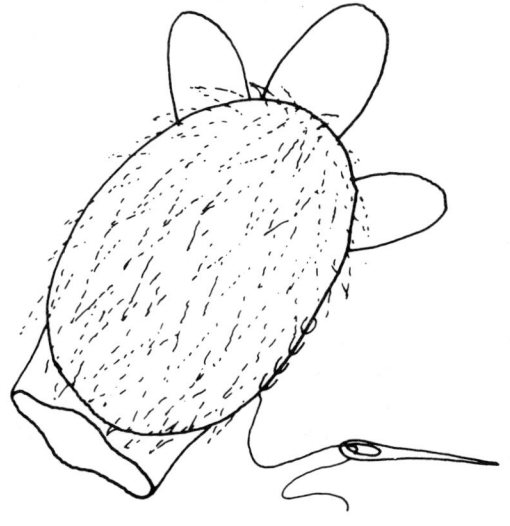

8. Glue or sew the fur piece **4** to the top of the head.

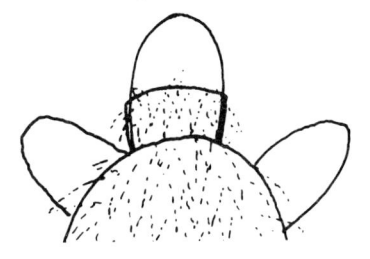

9. Sew the tail pieces **2** together leaving edge **A** open, turn right side out, and sew the tail to the body.

10. Glue the eyes and nose in place.

How to use

Put your hand inside him and wriggle his legs and head. Hedgehogs always curl up when anyone comes near, so touch him and then curl him up. Make him hibernate in a mound of leaves, cotton wool or bits of material.

● ● ● Mole

You will need

Black fur or velvet 15 x 22 cm
Black fabric 34 x 22 cm
Oddment of pink felt
Stuffing
Beads or sequins (for eyes)
Scissors
Pins, needles and cotton
Glue
Pencil and paper

Instructions

1. Enlarge the pattern to the right size on a piece of A4 paper and cut it out (see page 15).

2. Place the pattern pieces on the material as follows:
   1 on the fur or velvet
   2 on the fabric
   3 and **4** on the pink felt.

3. Pin in place and cut out one of **1**, two of **2**, four of **3** and one of **4** (see page 14).

4. Place the right sides of the hand piece **2** together and sew around the edges, leaving edge **A** open.

1. back

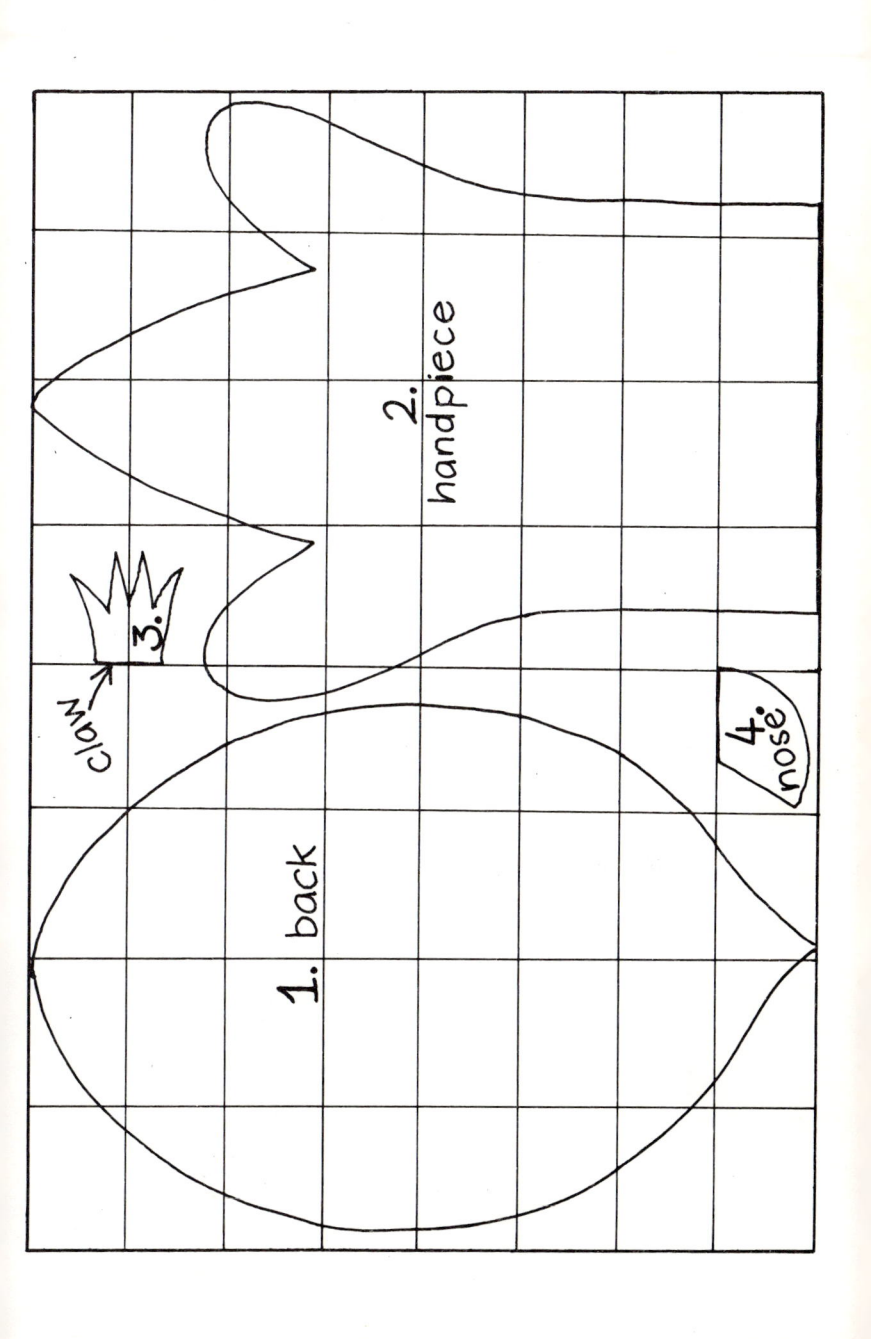

2. handpiece

3. ← claw

4. nose

5. Turn right side out.

6. Gather the fur piece **1** as shown to make it fit on to the hand piece leaving the legs and head free.

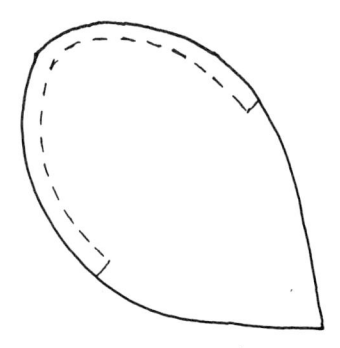

7. Sew the fur on to the hand piece (taking care only to sew through the top layer of the hand piece). Leave the pointed tail overlapping the edge as shown. Just before you finish sewing, stuff the fur slightly.

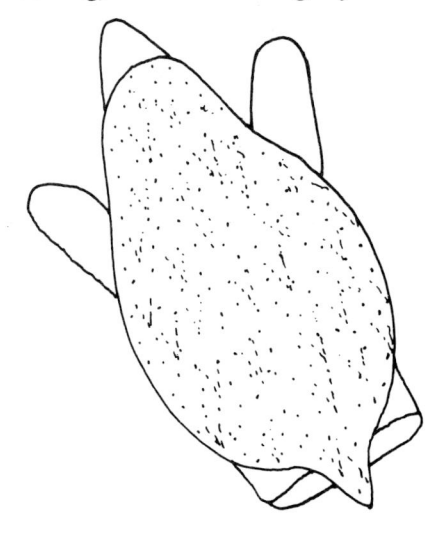

8. Glue the claws **3** on to the end of the legs.

9. Glue the nose into a cone shape and glue in position. Sew the beads or sequins in place for eyes.

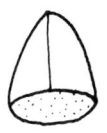

How to use

Put your hand inside and wriggle the mole's nose. Pretend to dig a tunnel and then pop him up for air – just like a real mole!

●●● Squirrel

You will need

Grey or red-brown fur 52 x 22 cm
Matching fabric
Beads (for eyes)
Black bead or button (for nose)
Stuffing
Scissors
Pins, needle and cotton
Glue
Pencil and paper

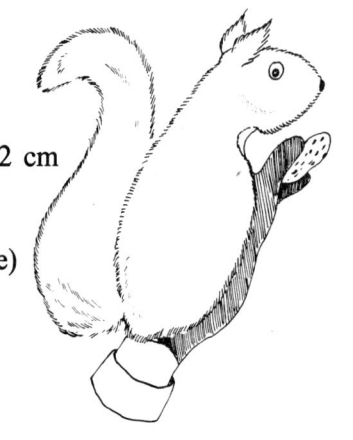

Instructions

1. Enlarge the patterns to the right size on pieces of A4 paper and cut them out (see page 15).

2. Place the pattern pieces on the material as follows:
   1, 2, 3 and **4** on the fur
   5 on the fabric

3. Pin in place and cut out one of **1**, one of **2**, two of **3**, four of **4** and two of **5** (see page 14).

4. Place the right sides of the hand piece **5** together and sew around the edges leaving edge **A** open.

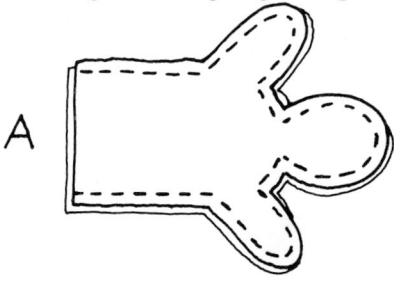

3. tail

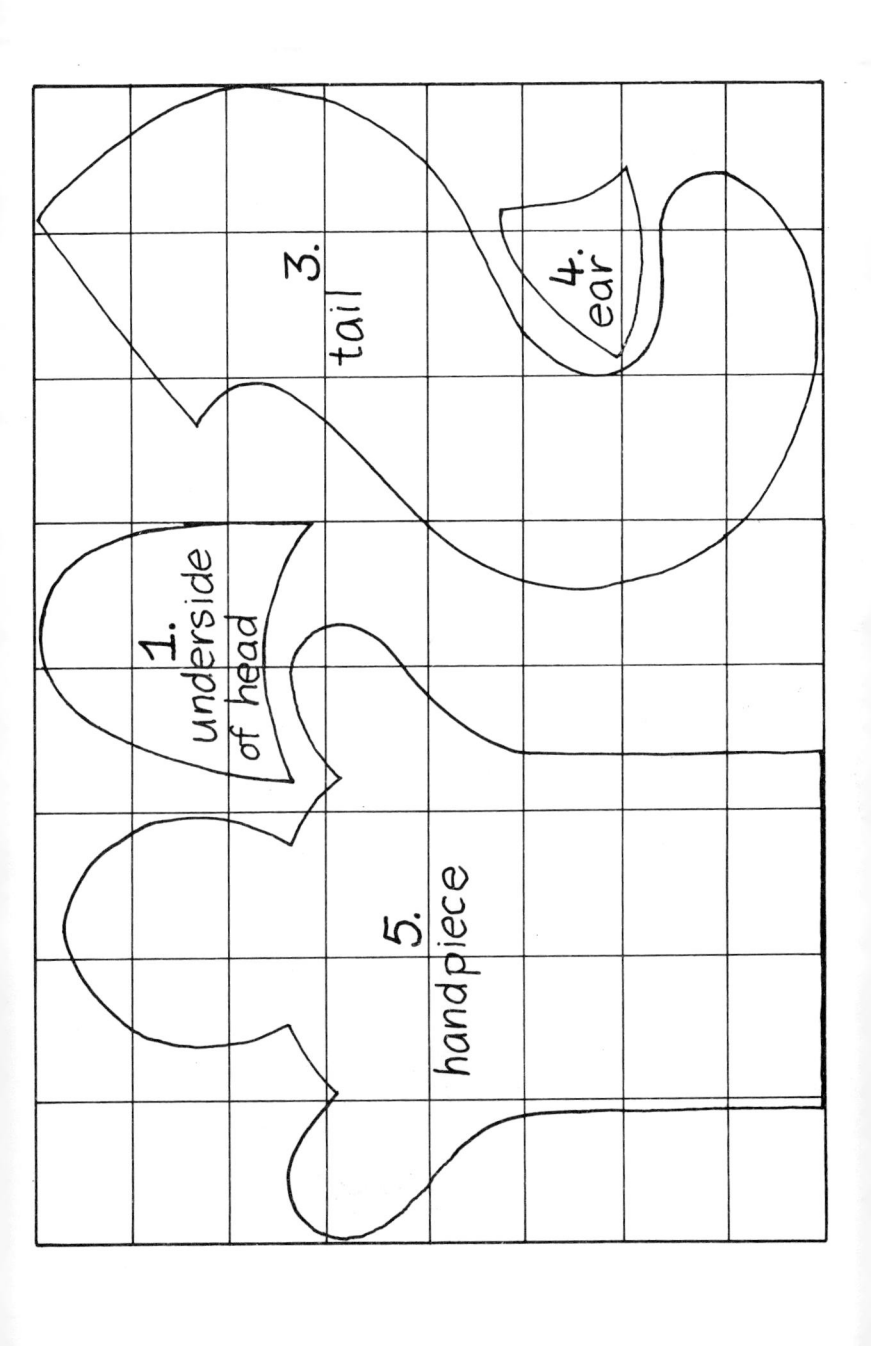

4. ear

1. underside of head

5. handpiece

5. Turn right side out.

6. Gather the fur piece **2** as shown to make it fit on to the hand piece leaving the arms free.

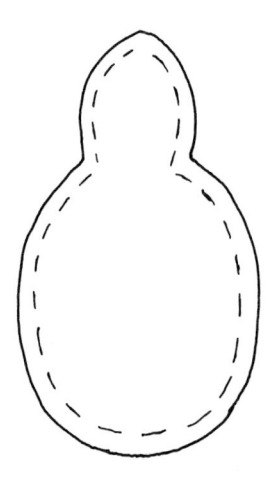

7. Sew the fur on to the hand piece (taking care only to sew through the top layer of the hand piece).

2. back of body and head

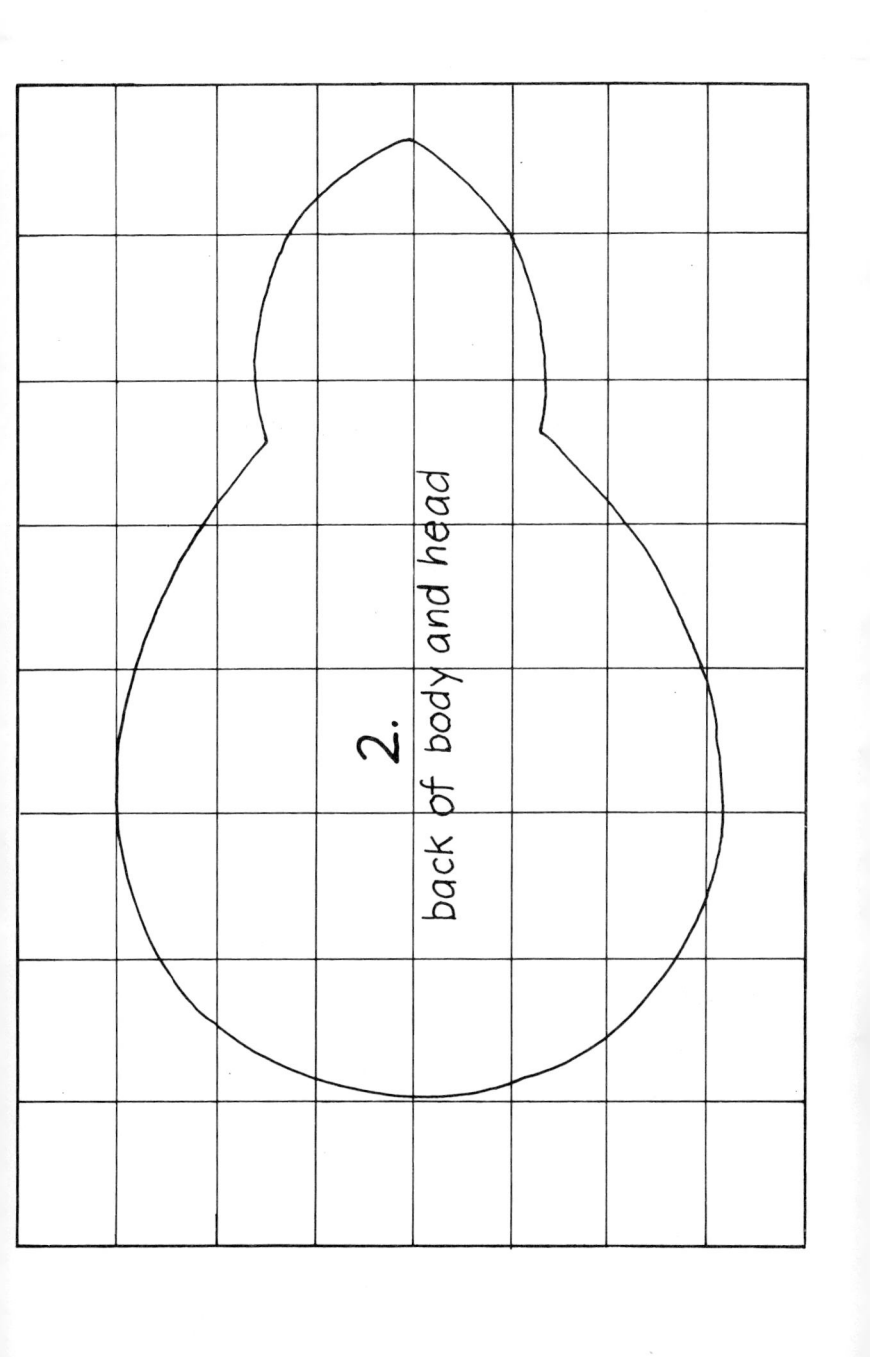

8. Sew on the underside of the head **1**.

9. Place the right sides of the tail **3** together and sew all around it leaving edge **A** open.

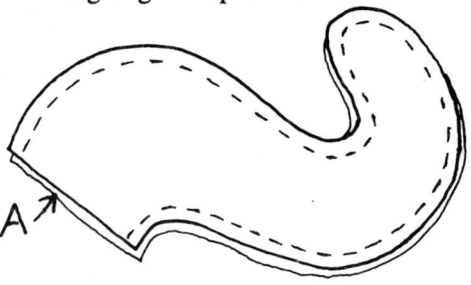

10. Turn right side out and stuff the tail.

11. Sew the tail to the body.

12. Glue the two sides of each ear together right side out. Then glue them in place on to the head.

13. Glue the eyes and nose into position.

How to use

Squirrels move fast, so make him run very fast up your arm. Hold a nut in his paws and nod his head, pretending he is eating it.

Stick Puppets

● Lipstick Baby

You will need

Old lipstick case (cleaned)
Pipe cleaner
Bead (for head)
Oddments of soft material or felt
Glue

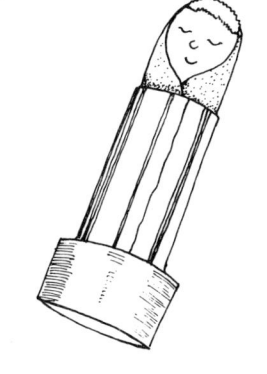

Instructions

1. Fold up the bottom of the pipe cleaner, and glue into the bottom of the lipstick tube.

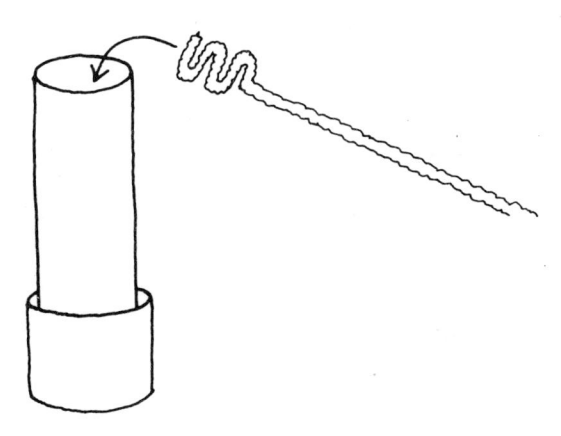

2. Cut off the surplus pipe cleaner. (Measure by swivelling the case right down, and cut pipe cleaner at this length.)

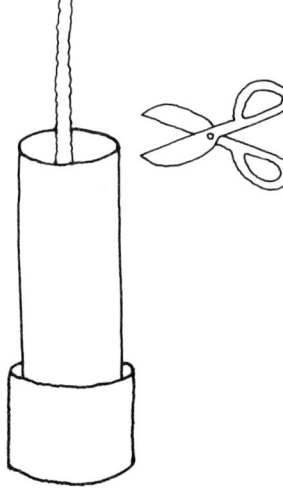

3. Bend the end of the pipe cleaner down by about 5 mm and glue the bead to the end.

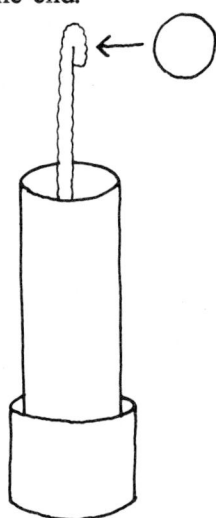

4. Drape some soft material around the pipe cleaner and head, like a shawl, making sure it fits inside the case.

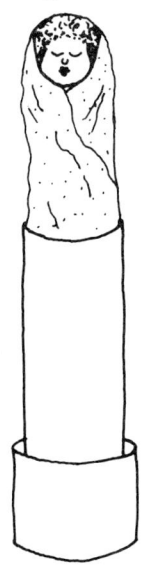

5. Glue into place.

6. Cut features from your material or felt oddments and glue into place.

7. Swivel the lipstick case down and put the cover on.

How to use

Take off the cover and swivel your baby into view.

Give him/her a name and find some baby rhymes to use.

● Crazy Spider

You will need

Polystyrene or ping pong ball
4 pipe cleaners
Oddments of coloured paper or felt
Thin elastic
Glue

Instructions

1. Make eight small holes in the ball for the legs.

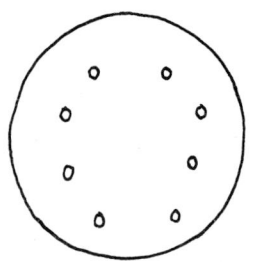

2. Cut the pipe cleaners in half. Push them into the holes and curl them slightly. Glue if necessary.

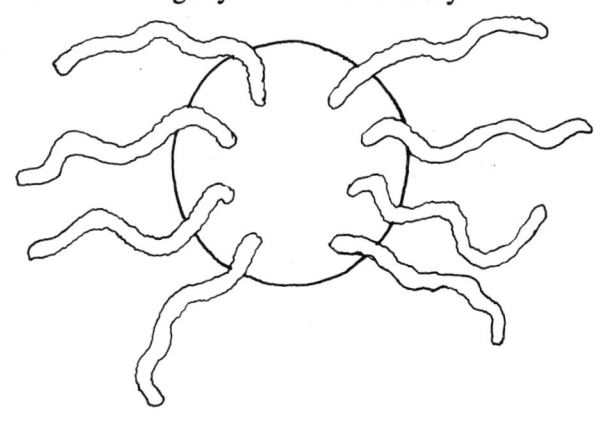

3. Make features from paper and felt and glue into place.

4. Tie a few knots on one end of the elastic. Make a hole in the top of the spider. Put in a spot of glue and push the knotted end of elastic into it.

How to use

When the glue is dry hold the elastic and bounce the spider up and down; or hang him up, give a little pull, and he'll do it on his own!

Scary Spider

If you want your spider to look more scary paint him black and use black pipe cleaners. Cut out his features from silver foil.

●●Safety Sticks

You will need

2 lolly sticks
4 pieces of red ribbon or wool 6 cm long
4 pieces of green ribbon or wool 6 cm long
4 small red buttons or beads
4 small green buttons or beads
Oddments of red and green wool
Glue
Red and green felt-tip pens

Instructions

1. Glue some red wool to the top of one lolly stick.

2. Draw on red eyes, nose and mouth.

3. Glue a red button or bead to the end of each piece of red ribbon.

4. Glue in place for arms and legs.

5. Now make a green man, by following the same instructions using the green materials.

How to use

Look for the red and green men on the crossing in town and make your men behave in the same manner.

Play games with your friends at home and practise crossing at the correct time: hold up the red man and your friends can't cross; hold up the green man and they CAN cross.

● ● Jester Spoon

You will need

Old plastic spoon or wooden spoon
Ribbon or wool
Felt-tip pens or paints
Glue
Coloured paper
Small bells (optional)

Instructions

1. Draw eyes, nose and mouth or cut out of paper and glue in place on to the round part of the spoon.

2. Cut a collar and hat to fit the spoon.

3. Cut the ribbon or wool into even lengths and glue under the collar at even intervals.

4. If you want your jester to make sounds when you shake him, sew some bells on to his hat or ruff.

How to use

Jesters are supposed to make people laugh, so do crazy things with him!

● ● Happy/Sad Mascot

You will need

Ball
Stick
Bell
Ribbons the colour of your team
4 goggle eyes
Oddments of felt and fur
Glue
Scissors
Wool

Instructions

1. Glue the stick to the ball, you may need to make a hole in the ball and push the stick into it slightly, before applying glue.

2. Cut out a ruff for the neck.

3. Glue in place by sliding up over the stick, and gluing to the base of the ball.

4. Cut the ribbon into eight strips.

5. Glue into place under the ruff.

6. Cut out two noses, one happy mouth and one sad mouth from your oddments.

7. Glue the features and eyes into place on opposite sides of the ball as shown. Glue on wool for hair.

8. To make the hat, cut out a large circle of felt (about 5 cm larger than the ball in diameter).

9. Decorate it with ribbon bands or colour with felt-tip pen.

10. Gather around the outside so that the hat fits the head.

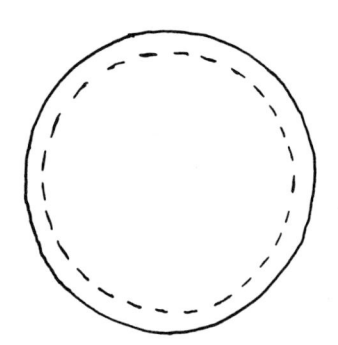

11. Put a bell inside and glue the hat on.

How to use

Take him to a game and show his happy face if your team scores or his sad one if the other team scores. Shake him and make his bell ring to encourage your team.

●●● Pop-up Baby

You will need

Small (one portion) milk/cream carton
Cocktail stick (with pointed ends trimmed off)
Small polystyrene ball
Oddments of felt, material and lace
Cotton wool
Glue

Instructions

1. Stick the end of the cocktail stick into the ball and glue into position.

2. Cut out a piece of material 8 x 8 cm.

3. Gather it at one end and glue around the neck of the ball.

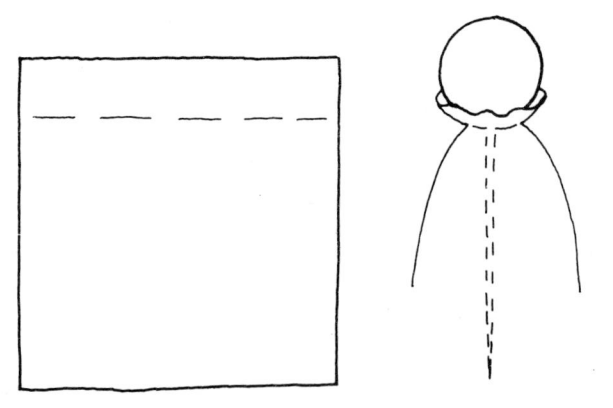

4. Make a hole in the bottom of the milk/cream carton and guide the cocktail stick through it.

5. Glue the bottom edge of the material to the outside of the carton.

6. Decorate the head with cotton wool hair and lace.

7. Glue on felt features.

How to use

Pop him/her up and down and surprise your friends.

●●●Chicken Inside an Egg

You will need

Bottom half of an egg box
Cocktail stick (with pointed ends trimmed off)
Yellow felt or yellow cotton wool balls
Oddments of felt
Sticky tape
Glue

Instructions

1. Cut two sections out of the egg box.

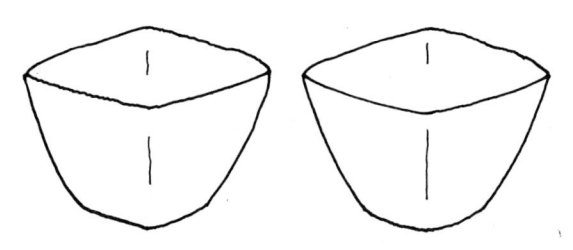

2. Cut out a chicken shape from yellow felt (or shape it out of cotton wool).

3. Make two eyes and a beak from oddments of felt and glue in position.

4. Glue the chicken on to the cocktail stick.

5. Attach the two sections of the egg box with sticky tape as shown.

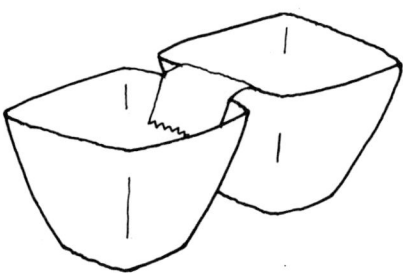

6. Open out the two sections and push the cocktail stick through the bottom one.

7. Close up your egg.

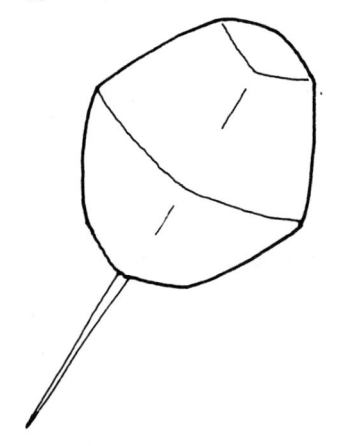

How to use

Push the stick up gradually and watch your chicken hatch out of the egg.

●●● Growing Flowers

You will need

Box, about 20 cm long,
  7 cm wide
Small (one portion)
  milk/cream cartons (preferably brown)
Plastic spoons
Oddments of felt and coloured paper
Large sequins
Wallpaper
Glue
Scissors

Instructions

1. Cut out two circles of felt about 1 cm in diameter for the centre of the flower.

2. Cut some felt or paper to make petals as shown.

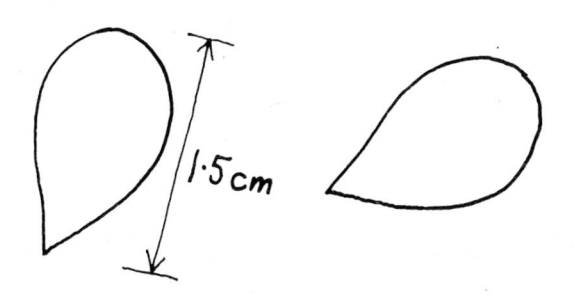

3. Glue the petals on to the centre of one of the circles as shown.

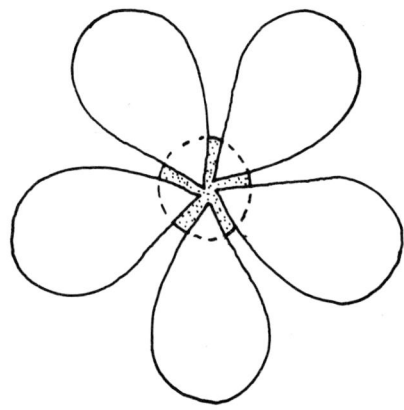

4. Glue the spoon to the back of your flower as shown.

5. Glue the other felt circle to the other side of the flower.

6. Make a hole in the bottom of the carton.

7. Push the spoon down through it.

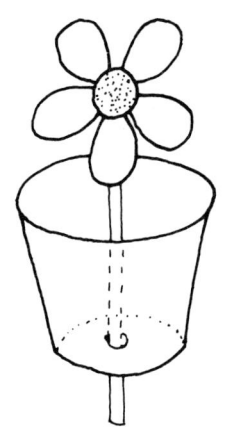

8. Make two more flowers in pots by following instructions 1–5.

9. Remove the lid from the box, you will not need this. Cover the box with wallpaper. (Try to find wallpaper with a brickwork pattern.)

10. Make three holes in one of the long sides of the box.

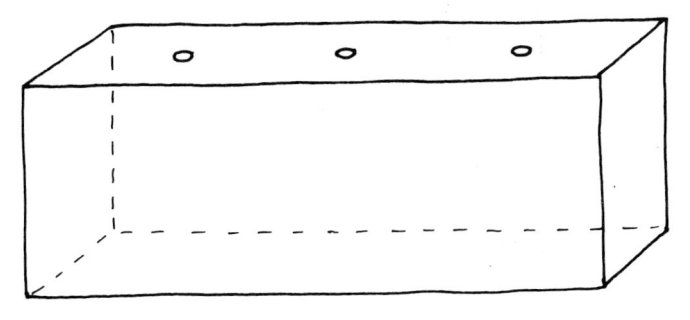

11. Glue the flowerpots to the box, pushing the plastic spoons through the holes in the cartons and in the box.

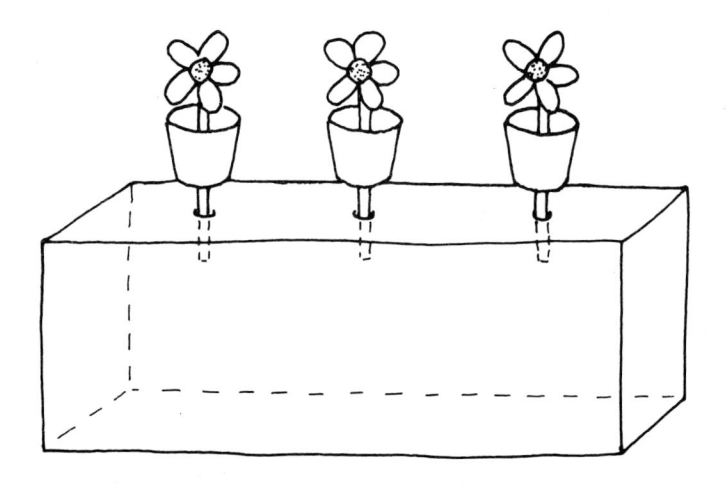

How to use

Make sure the open side of the box is facing you so that you can control your flowers. Push the flowers up and down in their pots and watch them grow.

●●●This Little Piggy

You will need

5 pots or cartons of different sizes
Box large enough to stand them on (cereal or shoe box)
5 balls of different sizes
5 pieces of thin stick
Pink material
5 bottle tops of different sizes
Pink poster paint
Oddments of felt
Card
Glue

Instructions

1. Glue a bottle top on to each ball to make the pig's snout.

2. Cut out ear shapes from card and glue them in place on each ball.

3. Cut out eyes and nostrils from oddments of felt and glue in place.

4. Push the balls on to the sticks and glue in place.

5. Paint your pigs' heads with pink paint.

6. Cut out a piece of material large enough to fit around the pot, and twice its depth.

7. Glue ends **A** and **B** together.

8. Gather the material end **A** and glue it around the pig's neck, drawing it in tightly.

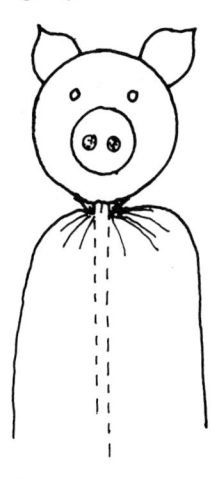

9. Make a hole in the bottom of the pot and guide the stick through, allowing the material to fall outside the pot.

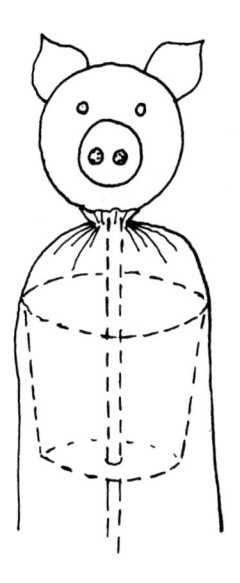

10. Glue the bottom edge of the material to the bottom edge of the pot.

11. Make four more pigs in various sizes, so that they range from the largest to the smallest in line along the top of the box.

12. Now follow instructions 9–11 on page 77. Decorate the box in any way you wish.

How to use

Say the nursery rhyme, 'This little piggy went to market,' and pop each pig up at the correct time.

Crazy Pigs

If you want your pigs to look even crazier, give them long hair made from wool. Then make them twirl around, with their hair flying everywhere.

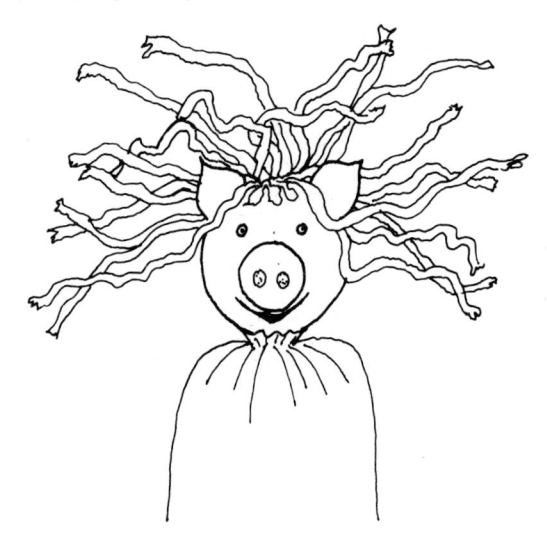

Walking Puppets

●● Humpty Dumpty

You will need

Round cheese box
2 pipe cleaners
Oddments of material and felt
Felt-tip pen
Glue

Instructions

1. Cut a half circle of pink felt, 1 cm larger than the cheese box.

2. Cut a half circle of another colour, 1 cm larger than the cheese box.

3. Glue these on to the outside of the cheese box lid.

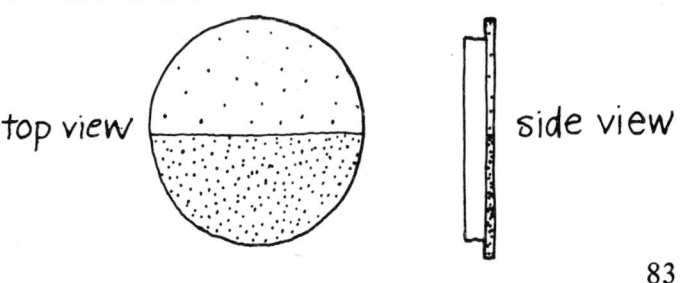

top view   side view

4. Glue the overlap down around outside of the lid.

5. Cut out two eyes, a nose and a mouth from the felt and glue these into place on the pink half of the cheese box.

6. Using different coloured felts, cut out a hat and a belt.

7. Glue these into place.

8. Bend the pipe cleaners in half and thread them through the sides of the box. Make felt hands and glue these to the ends of the pipe cleaners.

9. Cut two round holes in the bottom part of the box to put your fingers through.

10. Cut two pieces of felt 5 x 2 cm and two ovals as shown.

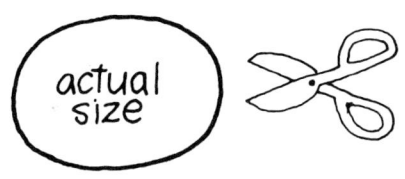

11. Glue the sides **A** and **B** of the strips together, to make a tube for your fingers.

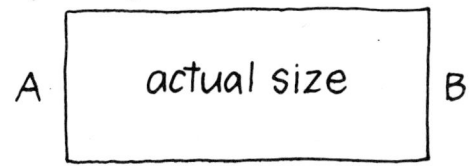

12. Glue a sole on to each. Now you have boots for your fingers.

How to use

Put your first and second fingers through his leg holes.
Put on his boots and make him walk, hop, jump and kick.
Sit him on your arm and pretend he is Humpty Dumpty sitting on a wall!

● ● Teddy

You will need

2 pieces of felt 12 x 8 cm
Oddments for eyes
Scissors
Glue

Instructions

1. Trace the teddy shape (see page 88), and using your tracing as a pattern, cut out one shape from each piece of felt.

2. Cut one shape in half as shown.

3. Glue the two top sections together.

4. Glue the edges of the legs together along the dotted line.

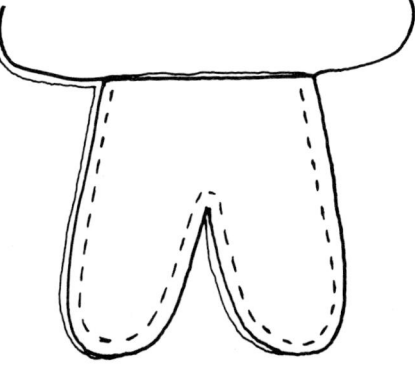

5. Glue the eyes, nose and mouth in place.

How to use

Put your fingers in Teddy's legs and make him walk.

Special Puppets

●● Pen Pal

You will need

Empty cotton reel
Ribbon or wool, 16 cm
4 beads or buttons
Oddments from Bitbox (for hair and features)
Pen or felt-tip pen
Glue

Instructions

1. Push the pen into one end of the reel, and glue in position.

2. Cut the ribbon or wool into four pieces and secure a button or bead firmly on the end of each piece. (Either thread through and tie in a knot or glue in position.)

3. Glue the pieces of ribbon or wool on to the reel, to make arms and legs.

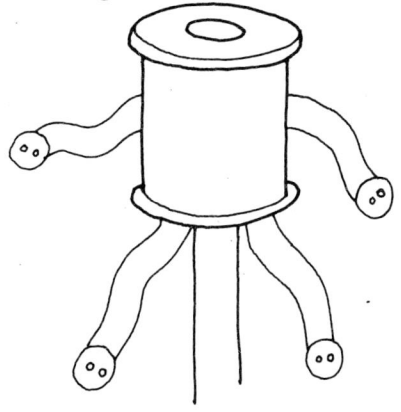

4. Cut out the eyes, nose and mouth and glue in place.

5. Glue a piece of fur on the top for hair and your Pen Pal is complete.

How to use

Twist your Pal around and make him click as he jumps about.

●●● Mischief the Cat

You will need

Long fur 45 x 45 cm
Pink felt
Oddments of felt
Large joggle eyes
Needle and cotton
Scissors
Glue

Instructions

1. Cut out two pieces of fur 15 x 30 cm.

2. Shape one end of each as shown.

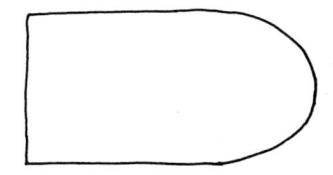

3. Cut out an oval of pink felt 10 cm long and 15 cm wide. Shape ends **A** and **B** so they fit the curved end of your fur piece exactly.

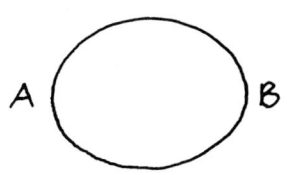

4. With the right sides of the fur piece together, insert the pink oval mouth piece.

5. Sew one half to the top piece of fur and the other to the bottom piece.

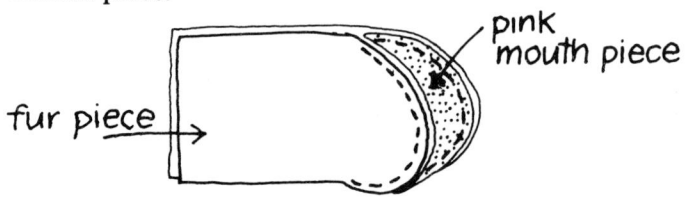

6. Sew the rest of the fur together – leaving edge **A** open.

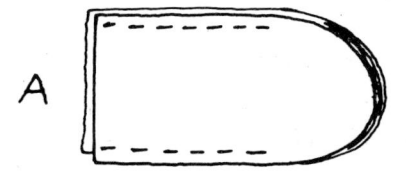

7. Turn right side out and push the felt inside to form the mouth.

8. Cut out a nose, ears and tongue from the oddments of felt.

9. Glue eyes, nose, ears and tongue into place as shown.

10. Cut a long narrow strip of fur for the tail.

11. Glue edges **A** to **B** with the right side outwards. Sew in position.

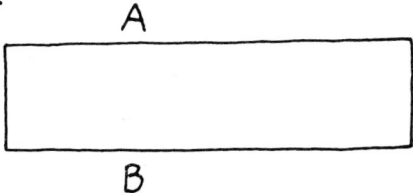

How to use

Put your arm inside with your thumb in the bottom of the mouth piece and your fingers in the top part. Open and close your fingers and thumb to make the mouth open.

If we call him Mischief we immediately expect him to be a naughty cat. Make him curl up on your lap or rest him on a table or armchair. Let him pretend to eat something. He also likes trying to catch his tail and hold it in his mouth!